CW00871934

Sonnets

Sonnets

Alan Prichard

ATHENA PRESS
LONDON

SONNETS
Copyright © Alan Prichard 2009

All Rights Reserved

No part of this book may be reproduced in any form
by photocopying or by any electronic or mechanical means,
including information storage or retrieval systems,
without permission in writing from both the copyright
owner and the publisher of this book.

ISBN 978 1 84748 523 6

First published 2009 by
ATHENA PRESS
Queen's House, 2 Holly Road
Twickenham TW1 4EG
United Kingdom

Printed for Athena Press

To
The Two Ladies of Sonnet 20
Both
Devotees
of
The Harebell and the Donkey
(Sonnets 90 and 136)

Preface

Few will be surprised that this collection of sonnets derives much of its inspiration from Shakespeare's peerless set. I hope they will not be regarded as a mere pastiche, but as an attempt to revive a form that seemed to fall out of favour with great poets who brought the English sonnet back into the Petrarchian rhyme system.

Sonnet No. 7 was written in the spring of 2004 as a thank you for the kindness of neighbours in providing a touching memorial for my then recently dead wife. The rest were all composed during 2006 and 2007 (in my mid-seventies) with the exception of No. 138, which was written in September 2008 on the occasion of a very dear friend's death. It is inserted next to No. 137, commemorating another equally dear John. The order is not predominantly chronological and there is no planned scheme for their arrangement, although particular sets tend to have been kept together and the last two obviously demand their location.

It will be seen I append certain notes (including a short disquisition on writing sonnets) after the sonnets. I would gently urge readers not to consult them until after they have read the whole set once, but the world will still revolve if that urging is ignored! Beyond this, I leave them all in the merciful hands of those who read them in the hope that they will enjoy them.

Sonnets' First Lines

1

There is a diseconomy of words
Which we ourselves do recklessly promote:
Some we debase like overgrazing herds,
Others o'ergild with sourly jarring note.
Such a one is dignity, fine virtue
Robbed too often of its endearing grace:
A stance that rich and mighty do pursue,
Hollow within, with false resplendent face.
But my love's dignity was never loud,
Just gentle, springing from her soul inside,
Meek, unassuming, and so far from proud,
Sweetly smiling, and honest till she died.
Like soft-hued garment was her dignity,
Kindly and traceless of malignity.

2

Here was a life that illness ravaged through,
Robbing her of much we take for granted;
A life debility unkindly drew,
Towards constant pain, distress, chagrin slanted.
An existence irksome, cabined, sore pent,
So difficult to bear and come up bright –
Angst over invitations kindly meant
By those who could not understand her plight.
Forecast to die in just six months was hard,
She gently told her surgeon and her nurse,
At age of seventy-two, but life marred
And death foretold at thirty-one, far worse.
Through all she lived a simple life of love
And put all her trust in her God above.

3

There is geography in all our living.
Vices and virtues form opposing poles:
Hard hearts incapable of forgiving,
Pleasure and fun dividing human roles.
Those who pleasure seek do blithely demand
As their right paramount priority,
Despising those who others understand
And pander not to their own vanity.
Pleasure inward looks, but fun sharing needs,
Equality, respect, all based on love.
My love and I found fun in simple deeds
And in and out a golden cord we wove.
Loving, cherishing, each to each best friend,
And we were playmates to the very end.

4

A marriage is much more than just a pair,
A survivor just a sorry fraction.
Two with harmony upright stand foursquare,
The blessed fruit of sweet interaction.
Arithmetic is stood upon its head
When human souls are integers in life:
Much stronger two alive than with one dead,
A husband wilts and fades without his wife.
One's achievements built on the other's strength,
No doer and spectator on this stage:
A partnership in depth and breadth and length,
Love's triumph painted on life's ev'ry page.
If I was seen to be the active one,
My weaknesses stand out now she has gone.

5

The happy husband knows that wealth he has,
Yet only in loss is the full score seen:
In loneliness one counts the debt there was,
How much was taken, and the gap between.
And now I ask why did she ne'er complain,
Bore my absence as I my works pursued,
She saw my success as her lonely gain,
Forbore to call it selfish attitude.
My grateful students sent their thanks to her,
Aware how much they owed her sacrifice.
The thanks I had we had earned together
And hers had been so much the greater price.
Thank God we had one joyous last decade,
But the debt I owed her remained unpaid.

6

She said she selfish was, and meant it so,
Throughout those long drear months of her decay.
We saw her courage, patience to and fro
Cross the trials and squalors of each day:
And for us all, consideration sweet,
And messages of love and deep concern ,
Which we observed no selfishness could meet
Or from our pain and love could ever turn.
She counted not the acts of love she did,
The kindnesses displayed to each and all,
So much of humble goodness that she hid,
Small acts of charity that were not small.
Failings to give and love did count with her;
And she was right: 'tis we that surely err.

7

A garden is indeed a lovesome thing:
What poet ever wrote a simpler truth?
There, joyous birds their sweetest phrases sing
And withered age recaptures bubbling youth.
Lady Camellia her soft glory shows,
Full pink of flower decking gloss of green,
While shy Euonymus one secret knows,
His leaves can match all else with varied sheen.
The dancing Fuchsia partners passing breeze,
Her red and blue do Nature's ballet score,
And lovely Nancy knows how best to please,
With full cream blossom from her buds of gore.
When zest in living sadly fades and ends,
Joy still lives on midst ever-loving friends.

8

Ranked with the grand and mighty was she not:
A simple loving life was all she craved,
Quietly helping, sweet'ning was her lot,
However roughly might her path be paved.
Pupils she taught, but friends would learn as much,
Such learning as would transfigure living,
Engendering delight and skill and touch,
Perfect epitome of self-giving.
Ne'er was impact so soft, and yet so sure,
And all responded in the selfsame kind.
The merits of such teaching e'er endure
When equal riches come to heart and mind.
For her 'twas love and gentleness held sway:
'Tis the prominent who have feet of clay.

9

True forgiving always involves a cost.
   A mild offence is easy to remit;
Not so, deep hurt to those that we love most:
Such culprits are much harder to acquit.
When creeping malice or bold callousness
Assaults our love and sears our very soul
And robs our heart of all its joyousness,
How comes forgiveness from our deepest dole?
Forgiving is, the poet said, divine;
Reviling, ire, recrimination sour
Can ne'er our erring, foolish hearts refine:
God alone can help us in such an hour
This my darling learnt and me taught so well:
Pray for the hurters – anger springs from hell.

10

All things will change unless a sweetness stays,
But often growth so far outvalues change.
What truly matters lasts for all our days,
Not passing fancies that our hearts derange.
Trawl far and wide and ne'er break the surface,
Passionate to taste all the world can give,
Terrified to slacken such sultry pace:
Thus chase experience, but never live.
The fear of losing out entraps the heart:
Just appetites all frantic'ly pursued,
No venue missed, sad rush that smothers art,
Leaving living crowded, crushed, curt and crude.
Do not by haste the simple wisdoms mar:
The shallow to the shallow shallow are.

11

A jigsaw puzzle is a marriage strong.
Each piece fits snugly in the other's soul,
And the puzzle grows as life wends along:
Pieces adhere as rings within a bole.
The puzzle neither edge nor corner needs,
Incidence and number prediction spurn.
Spouses rejoice as wayward pattern leads
And in the glory of each random turn.
To count and calculate sad errors are,
So wasting time for love and joy and fun.
On death of one the board is scattered far
And over half the tattered pieces run.
'Tis folly to try such loss to measure –
Only sorry fragments left to treasure.

12

Words are so precious and so bright and sweet,
    But too often so mindlessly misused,
Their meaning trampled under heedless feet,
With subtle shades appallingly abused.
Experts protest that language grows that way:
Yes, so it does, but growth can grossly flaunt
And sparkling words be turned to tarnished grey
When ignorance doth useful usage daunt.
'Anticipate', 'infer', and 'aggravate'
'Livid', 'demean', have their meanings stolen,
Other expressions just to duplicate,
Language cheapened and perversion swollen.
Waste not effort to rage, revile or swear,
Just shoulders shrug and shed a silent tear.

13

Oh! Pity those who blithely squander shame,
Morals are for losers, so they assert,
And see no damage in their cheating game,
Smoothly covering purity with dirt.
The eyes go preternaturally sharp,
Face lines are harder and the skin grows coarse.
Where others praise or soothe, they deign to carp;
Constancy they mock and contemn life's force.
They grab what pleases and ignore the cost,
The flesh their glory, and their belly god.
They think they win and see not virtue lost –
They downward rush at ev'ry devil's prod.
Relativism sets their poor souls adrift
Without the sense true happiness to sift.

14

What is true love? The age-old question chimes:
It is a pledge, a bond, commitment joint,
A self-surrendering 'cross place and times
Which solemn undertakings do anoint.
And yet – is it not simple, standing lone?
Still standing strong, regardless of return,
Trueness encamped within the lover's bone,
Needing no response for its light to burn?
With love returned the impact greater seems,
Yet, love's truer still with response denied:
The lover loves despite frustrated dreams
And loves on when that loving is defied.
Love's truth declines where's hint of selfishness:
To press one's love will make one's heart the less.

15

A dentist deft is multi-bladed Death,
Who draws life's tooth and leaves a yawning hole,
Forgetting not the mainspring root beneath,
Figuring the body, but e'en more the soul.
That gaping hole the longing tongue explores,
Aware the gap, yet seeking tooth to find –
Unreas'ning hope that batters fast-locked doors
And makes the heart reject the too clear mind.
The mouth persists to find a sweetness there
To turn aside the bitterness of grief,
Knowing the truth, but still intent to dare
To catch some soothing taste beyond belief.
We left behind do know our sweetheart gone:
Where once were two, is now but sweetless one.

16

No final judgement gives the finite mind:
  The burgeoning heart answer sole confers;
The finite stumbles, to true insight blind;
Unreas'ning reason judgement sound deters.
The faulty tool its fault can never see,
The haughty brain its compass overlooks,
The sceptic's dogmatism mislays his key,
Whate'er the weightiness of all his books.
Can the finite infinity reject?
Imperfection its own perfection claim?
Have wayward senses as their kings elect
Or rest upon the faultful framer's frame?
Whence spring potential and identity,
Save from the genius of Divinity?

17

Bereavement deals in simple pettiness:
The heavy blows a stalwart breastplate strike,
'Tis trifles that one finds so pitiless
And suddenly evoke the searing like.
Things little reckoned in our harnessed life
Revile proportion in our life alone,
As chance remembrance wields a stabbing knife
And gives the sweetest music sourest tone.
Remarks unthinking do mem'ries impart
And sounds and sights and smells and thoughts distract,
Recalling incidents with sudden start
When optimism collides with brutal fact.
And worst – news, quip, meeting, event to tell,
We find our listener's gone beyond the knell.

18

Grief's put on hold the while one's love still lives,
As unreality commands the mind
And, combating our good sense, hope yet strives
Against all reason, tossed by fancy's wind.
It is a time of rending helplessness,
Loving, caring, but all in tranquil mode,
Soft-muted in that dread, dying process,
The law of life receding by Death's code.
Aching paralysis our feelings grip,
Our loved one centre of our fading world,
We go through motions in our stewardship,
Fearing to show Death's banner all unfurled.
Mechanic'ly we carry out our role,
Dulled, useless in this Limbo of the soul.

19

If Death one's heart leaves scarcely moved, beware:
One's values and one's soul are commonplace.
In death alone is life's myst'ry laid bare
For us to ponder and its message face.
Here only can account be fairly formed,
With debts and payments beseeching balance,
Where virtues blossomed and our vices stormed,
For judgement finally evades all chance.
Sorrows and pain are too oft unfairly shared,
The good thereby to shoulder self-love's load;
But billing comes to see all debts are squared
And cynics grovel who once proudly rode.
Do not be sure the score will ne'er be paid –
The ink of Heaven does not ever fade.

20

I watched one dying and saw one aching,
Myst'ries in both beyond power to grasp:
A sweet gentleness I found heartbreaking,
Each victim of Death's daunting, cruel clasp.
The dying one so keen to soften loss,
The waiting one to wrap around in love:
Both finding words just useless, spongy moss
Where one flounders, trying one's love to prove.
The eyes and touch can part of message send,
But all's too deep for heart's impassioned pleas.
Who dies, who tends, each shares in loving end
To a marriage where love could never freeze.
My tears withheld, there occupied my mind
The gentle splendour of sweet womankind.

21

Judge not fast the reserved as tightly cold:
Some may indeed live with emotions drained,
But other some their timid hearts enfold,
Fearful the risks without their spirit chained.
Afraid offence to give as to receive,
They choke at unintended hurt or shame,
Terrified lest they realms of safety leave,
Expose a wildness they could nohow tame.
And yet, there's merit in their dignity,
Embarrassed not to cause embarrassment,
E'er striving to avoid duplicity
And bearing anguish to evade descent.
So do not readily such souls contemn:
Surely those that do, Heaven will condemn.

22

' Let there be light,' and light engendered lights,
And lights bejewelled our lives and minds and hearts:
The lights transforming all the lows and heights
And all the secrets that this world imparts;
The lights in water, pools, lakes and streams,
In silken textures, in human hair and eyes,
The lights that enthral, puzzle, shutter beams,
That speckle sunsets and deck dear sunrise.
One ev'ning such lights were all concentrate
Along Ullswater's sweetly straggling length,
Sun, clouded, could not colours overstate,
Soft, varied hues gave all a subtle strength.
Life whirls 'twixt sleek comic and rough tragic,
But Nature transcends with utter magic.

23

Whoever said that hearts grow cold with age?
That passions weaken and the blood runs thin?
That such must love desert and play the sage?
And never Cupid's prize aspire to win?
'Tis true the old do oft that saw believe,
Thus letting their loving powers decline;
While others do their systems sore aggrieve
And thus their lives and hearts so close confine.
But those who through life have others cherished,
And never ceased those others' needs to meet,
And recked not if their own interests vanished,
They will keep their powers of love full sweet.
For these blest creatures loving lasts for life,
Bemoaning those with inhibitions rife.

24

Seven deadly sins we know well there are,
Yet they are all just images of one:
That one is greed, which mocks the thought of share
And generates in one the heart of stone.
Adultery is greed, and so is sloth,
Pride too, and gluttony and drunkenness,
And stinking envy and unlovely wrath:
All give self more and leave one's neighbour less.
Greed arrogates beyond entitlement –
An arrogance which cheats and blackens soul
And leaves the record of one's dealing bent
And makes a sorry part where should be whole.
Say not 'tis private and betrays no trust:
Selfish dishonour merely trades in dust.

25

Words there are that gently love betoken,
Lacking any stressing of endearment.
They leave all such undertones unspoken;
So seems unromantic message sent.
Such a word is helpmeet, ne'er praised in song,
Down to earth, less e'en than companionate.
And yet – 'tis for a helpmeet I most long,
And with her loss I stand disconsolate.
She was my wisdom, beacon of sound sense,
Who loved too well to say me aye for nay,
Swift to bolster, to say when wrong intense,
With her my standards never slipped away.
All marriage has its glamour to maintain,
But honesty should be its rich refrain.

26

Few humans do the coming spring disdain,
For springs the heart as Nature self renews,
As winter's daylight yearning leaps again,
With snowdrops beckoning the season's hues.
My love the spring had always loved so much,
But deeper still when Death had summons sent,
Four decades back before its final touch:
Life savaged, yet spring's hopes full glory lent.
The haze of green ere hedges leaves did show,
Daffodils, primroses and violets,
Lambs frisking, birdsong, colours all aglow,
All sweetly banishing the thought of debts.
Her final wish, to die before spring came –
Too cruel to part from such splendid frame.

27

True measure of receipt is ever cost –
Distort it and our vision sadly fails.
'Tis when the focus of our love is lost
That we do find the balance in our scales.
Our love alive, 'tis true we freely give,
But such giving is one more gift to us;
Our love dead, 'tis then loving has to strive,
Intent upon our moral abacus.
Expanded heart new targets has to find
As vanished joys have left their debt to pay:
New aims for love must exercise our mind –
Less visible returns for us to weigh.
With our love gone, there is no trace of gain,
Yet solace may still lie within the pain.

28

Mean souls alone grieve not when friends depart,
For they are constituents of our life,
Their going amputation from the heart,
Howe'er gentle the handling of the knife.
Good sense for leaving can but part assuage
The ache of loss which does besiege our mind,
For friendship ever must exact its wage
Since by friends' warmth our spirits are refined.
That others now will have our fortune lost
Has to be our only consolation
When we do feel our paths with shadow crossed –
Our lives victims of sore violation.
Yet hope aids with promise of re-meeting
And that sweet thought keeps our hearts a-beating.

29

Equality of sexes is the rage:
Deny it and the pillory awaits.
But equality is an unjust cage
Which subtlety abhors and balance hates.
Equality doth fail to complement
And complementing is what love's about:
Equal each to each leaves true loving rent
And recognising need pent up in doubt.
Let not love strive unequal strengths to match
Or blind itself to where some take, some give:
Loving is seamless, not a patch for patch,
The other's weakness we must ease to live.
Unequal roles do harmony impart:
'Tis ev'ning up that grants the equal heart.

30

*Y*es, we were two, but so much more than two.
Each alone rarely single's best achieves,
But doubling more than doubles ones can do,
As lonely stalks show not the strength of sheaves.
Clean edges do not come with searing loss,
Nor confidence survive with uncut ease:
The bounce has gone when facing Fortune's toss,
Lost sheep struggling with sorry, tattered fleece.
Where once achievement stemmed from double strength,
Singles stumble on unfamiliar tracks
And mounting sorrow more than doubles length,
While Solomon shows how sadness attacks:
'Tis too easy to cast unwitting darts,
Singing joyous songs to sorrowing hearts.

31

Dost thou remember courtesy of old
When hearts weren't chained, nor smiles so close contained?
And consideration not deemed too bold?
And recognising kindness not restrained?
Chivalry requires not a Galahad,
Just hearts responding to another's need
And souls that suffer seeing others sad
And think not beneath them the kindly deed.
Equality will always bludgeon life
So long as gaze is upward fixed
And equalising feeds itself on strife –
Is care for others and for self fair-mixed?
Respect for others clears away self's debts:
'Tis justice that true courtesy begets.

32

True love ne'er looks within its powerhouse,
 Nor does it scan the bill this world presents,
Nor trim its flame for blind mankind to dowse,
Nor need a curtain wall its force to fence.
It can gentle go or find fastest pace.
Confined, it withers: freed, it bounds full fast.
Faults it scorns to probe; weakness tastes its grace,
With sweetness exorcising wilting past.
The lover's self tightly it must ignore,
The other's self above all else exalt,
Confident it will ne'er exhaust its store,
Nor let worldly wisdom impose its halt.
All else in life submits to finite bounds:
Love endlessly expands its flowing wounds.

33

Honest love knows not itself, nor seeks to bind,
But pours out itself, keeps no force in hand,
And savours morsels which it sweet will find:
How can the one so loved such love withstand?
The loving heart defies predicted burst
And feels no need to buckle armour on,
Disdaining ev'ry chance to slake its thirst,
And ne'er perceiving when all hope is gone.
Broiling hot, then icy cold, ne'er lukewarm,
Pulse racing, slack'ning with the loved one's frown,
Rebounding hard in face of smiling charm,
Ne'er damp'ning throbbing aspiration down.
If, 'spite of all responding, love comes not
The honest lover ne'er bewails life's lot.

34

Corrupting power is no novel thought,
Its taste enslaving and its lure so strong:
Never the victim the sole actor caught,
Both drowning in the malefactor's wrong.
Sage Acton spelled the sorry lesson out
For power absolute, but gentler spoke
Of power less free: yet the urge to flout
Grows fast with knowing how abuse to cloak.
Unearned trust and apathy encourage
Midst a public reluctant to mistrust –
A baying, sycophantic entourage
That fawning bolsters power-holders' lust.
Unflagging vigilance needs something more –
A healthy shrewdness at the people's core.

35

Rare mysteries can agonise us all
When life confounds the surest of beliefs
And leaves us gasping in doubt's toughest thrall
And scepticism cannot confer reliefs.
It was a journey I so oft had done,
Knowing the road as well as any might,
And knowing too how safe a speed to run
And not to follow with a margin tight.
I'd hoped a modest pace would be my lot,
An expeditious journey, dangerless:
Instead, a madd'ning dawdle, cramping trot,
Reason thwarted in this pilgrim's progress.
What stupefaction for a driving man
To be stuck behind a sedate white van.

36

' Love thy neighbour as thyself,' says the law:
A simple precept to the lazy ear,
That makes no sense to hearts that cannot thaw
Or have a pallid concept of what's dear.
What would we truly from our neighbour wish?
A bare equality, or something more?
Strict balanced measure on a formal dish,
Meagrely eked out from a grudging store?
Generous response to our need we crave,
Uncalculating, prompt and freely warm
With cost uncounted whate'er one might have,
The love and kindness of the unloosed arm.
This law can no exception recognise:
Despise it, and civilisation dies.

37

Unpredictable how long grief will last:
Each soul explores its rending depth and length.
Forewarnings apt can grant a vague forecast
And hint of misery's slow tread and strength;
But each soul works it through and makes its map,
With mental markers of its searing pain,
Surprised to find the battered heart not snap
'Spite constant blows from death's enduring reign:
The numbness of the early months or weeks
Replaced by fuller agony of loss,
Then plunged deep in gaunt loneliness's creeks,
As severance claims its drear right to boss.
Grief's gradual retreat will linger on,
Leaving a void with all our sweetness gone.

38

The finite mind the finite only grasps:
Infinity for him is fairy tale;
Mathematics – fool – a foolish symbol clasps,
For finite minds insist such symbols fail.
For all such minds the finite is their god,
Lulled by language which shirks infinity,
Departing not from ways their tongues have trod,
Content to spurn unseen divinity.
They look no further than their senses prompt,
Dismissing whole and substituting part.
Joyful in playpens where they always romped,
Claiming omniscience from their wheel-less cart.
The tragic fault, rejecting Lord above,
Is thereby so closely to limit love.

39

To love unloved doth crush the staunchest heart
And paralyse emotions sweetly dear
While nearness stresses sharp the gap apart
And all love's finery dies fiercely drear.
I've known bereavement, felt its deathly chill,
Harsh currycomb scratching at inmost soul,
Stealing away all spark and cheering will,
Forlorn embers fanned from blackest coal.
Love unreturned does not evade such pain:
Bereft by death the gnawing blade bites deep;
Love living, stubborn hopes so sore remain
And constantly the dismal insights keep:
The chilling heat from passion's grimmest stove
And measured tread of unrequited love.

40

Ever the wishful heart its dreams sustains
'Spite ev'ry message that the brain receives:
True love, outlawed, surrender still disdains,
Though love ne'er re-springs from dead, trampled leaves.
E'en when the loved one bears no trace of guilt,
Bitterness inward turned can grow apace
Unless one's loving was on sweetness built
And still avows her beauty and her grace.
The questing heart will ask and ask and ask,
Refusing to be reconciled with loss,
Yet desperate the aching pain to mask,
Knowing rejection is a cruel boss.
Time heals, they claim, but tender hearts know well
Such waiting time is still a dragging hell.

41

True loving must full enterprise embrace,
Overspilling and never close confined,
Transmitting joy unto the sadder face,
Both outward looking, not to others blind.
That sacred pledge that marriage has to be,
Golden bond, society bewitching.
It starts with two who make a glorious we,
Then outflows, humanity enriching.
Spouse and family do comprise love's well,
But love conserved is sadly harnessed,
Sours when it any other doth repel:
The love expanding is the one that's blessed.
Think not that love is good when it exults
Unless there's none excluded from its cults.

42

Best of metaphors is the human heart:
It throbs, it pulses, floods a system whole;
It firmly sets the brain – and mouth – apart,
Figuring the love that sparks the soul.
A simple pump it is, the experts say,
Internal, invisible, e'en mundane.
Face, head, shoulders, emotions do betray –
The joy, the mirth, the ire, the pride, the pain.
Yet, dull heart enslaved the human race,
Became the darling of poetic minds,
Ranging feelings from fine to plainly base,
As each one his favourite symbol finds.
Can there be any image quite so fine,
Providing poets with so rich a mine?

43

Mothers thought me splendid, daughters not.
Years later, girls warmed to such charms I owned,
But equal age preferred the cold to hot
And left my loving sore dethroned.
One can be liked, one can be sweetness shown,
Yet ne'er evoke the slightest trace of love,
Making my charmless person me bemoan –
No soaring eagle I, just pallid dove.
Just once – with time – I did a love evoke,
A love much richer than my dreams could spell,
Which for a while my inhibitions broke,
Bathed at last in Aphrodite's well.
But how that hard-won confidence sustain,
When once again one finds one loves in vain?

44

My heart was sunken and my spirits bleak,
Patrolling the height, then tracking the shore,
Lake water ruffling in a gentle creek,
Sunlight and breeze opening heaven's door.
When nature sparkles, wounds intensify
And beauty underlines unhappiness,
Prompting deep joy until the magic die
And sorrows all the sweetnesses suppress.
Golden evening mocked evening of my life,
For fire can cheer, but fire can also scorch.
With loss compounding age with achings rife –
Beware the wind that that forces back love's torch.
So, strolling there I had too much to muse:
Earth's glory will elate, but knows how to bruise.

45

*E*ach soul marches or staggers on its way
  In face of loved one's death as it responds
With calculation, or come as it may,
Midst wilted flowers and withered fronds.
Three sharp queries beset the mourning heart:
How now to direct one's rich store of love?
And how its stolen richness to restart?
And how the sick'ning motionless to move?
Loving that burgeoned now has lost all scope,
Facing an emptiness one cannot fill,
Knowing cruel death has slain sweetest hope,
Yet lover knows love started must love still.
True love must never full loving forgo,
But whom to love only true love can know.

46

Spread butter thin, you'll have a life of dough:
Narrow the soul, the heart will shrivel too.
Snatch pleasure now and garner future woe –
Chances loving to expand come too few.
Smiling alone is pleasure close confined,
Sharing and response make our living rich:
Pleasing self alone surely sets the mind,
Producing music at its lowest pitch.
Love self and render self unlovable:
To pamper others takes a foolish risk,
To pamper self does your love disable,
However much you feel your heart awhisk.
When life rides high you'll feel no need to love;
When life descends there'll be no hearts to move.

47

Strange how foreign words can entrance the tongue:
'Elan' is one that surely proves that point –
Uplift, joy, drive, excitement's bell hard rung,
All fail its special essence to anoint.
No language can ev'ry nuance capture
Or find apt term for each phenomenon
Or form the very word to enrapture.
Words do suggest, but the true sense has gone.
No synonym or e'en apt metaphor
Can bottle up its richly bubbling sense
Or reach into its effervescent core,
Conferring freedom on the sadly tense.
Without élan, spring to the winter turns:
E'en truest love to bitter ashes burns.

48

Set not your heart on things of second rank,
Nor let your life wander from truest joy,
Obsessed with monies growing in a bank,
Besotted with the evanescent toy.
Yes, shelter, food, drink, clothes we surely need
And sense ordains we labour for enough,
But concentration is a cruel creed:
Seek not the smooth, only to find the rough.
Do not augment the cares that come in life
By thinking safety best lies in excess:
Recall instead too much engenders strife –
Take more than needed, others have the less.
Measure your soul, in that alone lies sense:
Be ever prudent in your providence.

49

Hug not your love to self, lest it reduce,
For we are trustees of that golden gift.
Let not its glory its purport seduce,
Lying flat when it all is meant to lift.
The spouse, the loved one, holds the pride of place
While children and the family press close,
But there's a world that's starved of loving grace
And so rarely its healing power knows.
Real love a springboard ever needs to be
So all may feel its richness and its bounce:
Spouses their love cement imparting glee
And joy and showing how their loving counts.
Love most abounds and brightens human life
When it springs out from 'twixt husband and wife.

50

Oh, pity those who love asudden find,
For loving loves from out itself to grow:
Its practice can alone instruct the mind
And so permit the inner knowing know.
Love crushed – or bruised – the quest is handicapped:
A home's best breeding ground hearts to expand,
Where loving instinct is not harshly snapped
And nascent youth well knows the loving hand.
For love's a discipline one must cherish
Where whole-heart giving grants its dividend,
With meanness scorned and bestowing lavish
And to heartlessness never to descend.
When home its loving kindness has well made,
Love's cost is nothing, for its price is paid.

51

The broken heart begets the richest hoard,
For love unchallenged ne'er demands a bill,
Content to savour its so sweet accord,
Not weighing as it takes its gleaming fill.
Clear but brutal is the message loss tells,
When love is forced a lonely lane to take
And itching hope harsh reality quells –
How then tormenting thirst can lover slake?
How measure value unless payment's made?
Only suff'ring souls can weigh sadness' cost –
Or judge the joint from off the butcher's blade
When all the joy and sweetness has been lost.
Connoisseurs can judge the desert's beauty:
Lovers know their pain to be their duty.

52

Underrate not the unrequited love,
Nor think the truest heart will quickly mend,
Write off the wasteland of love's blighted grove,
Or lover's misery not comprehend.
Broken hearts bereaved, broken hearts unloved
Are sister passions in our human woe,
Pitiless in emptiness blankly proved,
Cruel absence, the unrelenting foe.
Blest those who never feel its burning hurt,
But blessing meagre it may truly be
For burn can purify of selfish dirt
And leave the heart from inward feeling free.
The lover to unhappiness consigned
Knows well his aching heart must be confined.

53

Joy once I knew: then time did never hang,
And life did sparkle, easily smiles came,
And ev'rywhere the sound of laughter rang
As if my birth had come from Fortune's Dame.
Love lost, arrived flat pain and emptiness,
Soul robbed of sweetness and bereft of mirth:
Each day's ambition to be more heartless
And to revel in joyfulness's dearth.
Great art exults in pointing up contrast,
But proud agony stands unrelenting,
Coarsely reviling love's glorious past
And its dear confidence crudely denting.
But through it all I ever strive to cheer,
Knowing folk will think I am happy here.

54

'Twas the Louvre where delight came my way:
  I wandered spellbound in its splendid thrall
Till hit by magic – light-dark interplay
Responding to Nature's sublimest call.
Caravaggio my heart and mind had won
And Honthorst too I was very soon to know;
But de la Tour enchantment specially spun,
Letting darkness the truest light to show.
Highest art the cardsharpers demonstrate,
But announcing angel and Virgin taught,
Catching the sad Magdalen contemplate
And Child with Joseph deepest truth have caught.
Darkness with light, nothing trite, nothing dour,
Such is the legacy of de la Tour.

55

Most nice people do inferior feel,
And it is good that they do feel that way;
For they in doing down do never deal,
Wishing the rules of kindness to obey.
The brash one talent have – to push ahead:
Others to them are objects to surpass,
Drawn magnet-like to stand in leaders' stead
So worldly bonus points they may amass.
Bonhomie for them solely is a tool,
With self-aggrandisement their narrow end
And self-sacrifice marking out the fool
And useful contact their idea of friend.
Worry not then you so deficient are,
Thrusters' success their natures e'er will mar.

56

When I do marriage deeply contemplate
Humour's 'better half' filters to my mind:
Despite the triteness and its smiling fate
It imparts a meaning that is just and kind.
Unless one finds one's mate the better soul
One kills the confidence a marriage needs
And risks that marriage ever being whole
And doubts and hesitations sourly seeds.
Each one must for a complementing strive
And through each other's strengths achievement win,
Finding fulfilment in their mutual drive,
With weaknesses heaven's ushering in.
As man and wife we'll play, we'll sing, we'll laugh:
Best of all, she'll be my bettering half.

57

When life becomes a sorry trod of woe
And nothingness besieges wounded heart
And all that's fair turns into fiercest foe
And sweet mem'ries have all learnt how to smart,
Then lead replaces love's own ore of gold
And drags where once the pace was fleet
And glitt'ring dreams to emptiness are sold
And bitter tastes usurp the soothing sweet.
Then love's dignity its dread hour must face
And keep its gnawing pain within itself,
Though every meeting robs the heart of grace,
With Fortune's fairy turned to malign elf.
All this the sorrower so sadly bears,
Smiling and laughing through smarting, unshed tears.

58

Live in the present, that my loved one taught:
The past we can recall, but ne'er call back;
Future's for dreams and plans, of sureness nought,
Today is when human trials attack.
Learn from the past, yes, but only gently,
And ne'er live within its custody;
Ponder tomorrow, but ne'er intently:
Spirit ever must respect the body.
For body's time is now, and only now,
And all good deeds occur within its time,
And evil doings find such time enow:
'Tis there we choose the rainbow or the grime.
Blame not the past nor promise future good,
Be kind today and savour Heaven's food.

59

The humble find infinity sure sense:
Only the proud baulk at its dominance
And seek their insights in their own pretence
And will not yield their guarded prominence.
A God they loathe for robbing them of pride
And making thus their reason tumbledown,
With imperfection's solitary guide,
Deeming wider horizon overgrown.
While gentler minds see end in endlessness
And are content not everything to know
And feel no shame when called upon to guess
Where conscious limits can full sense not show.
Seek no evidence in brilliant gene:
Its brilliance comes from power unseen.

60

Lazy minds deal not in circumspection:
They prefer their self-chosen starting point,
Hope their prejudice escapes detection,
So they may their pre-eminence anoint.
But reason seeks no kingdom on its own,
Acknowledges it only wisdom serves,
Disdaining any academic throne,
And softly, subtly pretension unnerves.
It is merely conclusion's walking stick
Along the path of truest scholarship,
Content to be the mind's flickering wick,
Aware so often of the cruel blip.
Reject not the heart's sound explanation,
There is no answer save in creation.

61

How I yearn for a twosome once again,
That blessed pairing that engenders drive,
With energy that stimulates the brain
And keeps one's better instincts full alive.
There's no extravagance in such a bond,
One simple word, one single smile suffice:
No flow'ry gestures telling we are fond,
Laboured once surrend'ring to blessed twice.
Gaps in confidence and in sure response
Melt away with one loving, sweet caress;
And there is light again within the sconce,
So bleak despair gives way to happiness.
My soul doth ache for what my life once had,
Leaving me sadly mad – and madly sad.

62

What is it that women really desire?
Some, no doubt, wealth, power, or even ease,
Others a fuller, deeper life require,
Never letting their loving nature freeze.
Even they hints of heady glamour crave
Beyond what they just count as solid worth.
Kindness, thoughtfulness they would gladly have,
Tenderness too, and courtesy and mirth,
But most of all the feeling they are prized
And set apart from other womankind,
With subtle flattery never despised:
My love, I wager, owns a better mind.
Her I would have my darling Princess be:
Sadly, there is no trace of Prince in me.

63

Time has gone on, not fast, but steadily.
Each soul works out its own bereavement's pace:
Friends' comfort and support come readily,
And yet, there still remains the empty place.
I've seen the searing pain of the bereaved,
The dread rape of ability to give;
But my loss was with sweetness interleaved,
Her gentle legacy all positive.
'Twas her behest that I should cheering keep,
Hugging not our loving possessively,
Spreading its wealth with true measure deep,
And overall, like her, so sensitively.
Hers is a wisdom fondly sacrosanct,
But cloaked anguish stays by the world unthanked.

64

Suppress sly urges to appear mature:
Sophistication charges dire returns
And renders tawdry e'en sweetest nature,
Leads to the desert where all merit burns.
Stand back to survey and learn lesson clear:
Vying to surpass, falling sadly short,
Thrusting the trivial, repressing the dear,
Gilding the tinsel, freshness to abort.
Peer pressure robs sweet innocence and youth,
All in the quest of seeming superior,
Blind to the sin of prostituting truth,
Becoming – as hollow wage – inferior.
Humanity rarely loves artifice:
There are much better ways to win true bliss.

65

Why does mankind so oft paint wisdom grey,
As if all humour and light touch detract,
And deep thought must advance on stony way
And jest is alien to revealing fact?
Satire and irony may be allowed
So long as there's a worthy, measured tread,
As if laughing offends the heavy-browed
And smiling subverts the sound-thinking head.
Does true reason really gaiety flee,
While great thinkers brains armour-plated sport,
Chuckling only outside their library,
Fearing their scholarship will be held short?
Although all wisdom brings a harvest rich,
The wisdom's surer when the grey beards twitch.

66

A simple peasant, poverty's own child,
A background ripe to spawn indignant wrath,
Yet staunchly she remained intently mild
And ne'er abandoned Heaven's stony path.
She believed and, believing, would not budge
And knew her vision was holy, good and true;
Rose above what sceptics and cynics judge,
And gently, firmly stuck to what she knew.
Broken soldiers her no wonder treasured,
And former doubters became acolytes:
Her sweet courage was in patience measured
With bleak days merging into breathless nights.
Deepest love was ever in her touch:
The non-achiever who achieved so much.

67

A curious concept is dignity,
Elusive to discerning intellect
And owing nothing to rigidity,
And so much more than holding self erect.
The proud and haughty see it as their own,
Never ascribing any to the humble,
Seeing it sit on their exclusive throne,
Confident their kind can never stumble.
And yet true dignity must never hurt,
Coming from the heart, not from any stance,
Dealing in kindness, aloof from pride's dirt,
Ever intent dear virtue to enhance.
Beware: unless there's warmth in dignity,
It will be rooted in iniquity.

68

Pity the men of undoubted talent
Who all too easily attained the heights,
Blunted awareness of what virtue meant
And kept advancement clearly in their sights.
Manipulation was their favoured game,
Fawning on the sadly second-rate,
They inheriting, not themselves, the shame,
Confident they were masters of all fate.
Unthoughtful arrogance was their reward:
Crushed victims were the price they blithely paid.
Malice, not love, became their master card,
Unaware they'd made all sweetness fade.
Ambition's avalanche advanced their sway
And thus they lost the brightness of the day.

69

Whenever friends you wisely seek to choose
And to tie bonds that seem sound sense to make,
Beware lest other souls you thereby lose
And thus good friendships all unthinking break.
Friends need an active, outward-thinking haul,
Ensuring their friendship grows well apace,
Excluding no one, but enriching all,
And never confining one's smiling face.
This for my country I would dearly wish,
A springboard for others to join our band,
Not be excluded from our loving dish,
But ev'ry human our best friend to stand.
From humanity much Europe's taken:
Select, then rightly you will be forsaken.

70

We die the thousand deaths lest we offend:
Embarrassment stifles the loving heart,
Leaving our kindness so intensely penned,
Thrusting our caring into wheel-less cart.
How oft we fail encouragement to give,
Fearing our genuineness will not shine through,
Forbidding generosity to live,
Letting convention give life darker hue.
Fears of rebuff excuse not sad meanness,
Reddened cheeks should never warmth inhibit,
Nor rob charity of golden keenness
Or promote the strangling of the spirit.
Never repress calls of loving instinct:
Shortfalls in love with sin are tightly linked.

71

Caution and love a constant battle fight,
Tearing apart frail timid hearts,
As if afraid to yield to dazzling light,
And fearing to o'ercome whatever thwarts.
Free will is splendid till entrapped by doubt,
Then choice becomes hell-begotten torment,
Soul robbed of power to cast doubting out,
Content to leave all fine feelings dormant.
But inner self should tell shrinking ensues
And leaves the soul a pallid, weakling thing
That nothing blest or lasting e'er imbues
And bars the spirit's ever taking wing.
Choose love to fight to conquer all:
Build not around you just a prison wall.

72

I never met her, never picture saw,
Never heard her voice – I knew so little;
Yet, I knew her beyond bland nature's law
And thrilled at her life, so fine, so brittle.
Beyond brave youth death's call strikes the sourer,
As if lost chances augment fears of loss
And dying is cleanser not, but scourer,
And our achievements shine as tawdry dross.
My heart aches to see life's span so severed,
A life so short and yet so richly full,
Brave striving through all that she endeavoured,
Wholly positive, scornful of death's pull.
And we, the old, so short in loving deeds,
See in young life and death what goodness heeds.

73

Just five of us came to Our Lady's shrine,
Three first timers, two our joy renewing.
We hoped thereby our souls we might refine,
From gently paths of sweet faith pursuing.
Mary's reward was friendship from the South,
Though few from there would Southern extract claim,
A jolly, holy band, with timeless youth,
From whom an ever-ready smiling came.
Ne'er did they hesitate us to enfold
With all the love and care of truest friends,
Sharing with us their moments of fine gold,
Freely giving what love comprehends.
To come to Lourdes is ever privilege:
That much more with dear friends from Stalybridge.

74

He was the eldest of us brothers four,
In worldly terms the least successful was.
Fate did not deal to him an easy score
Such as an eldest the most often has.
Eighteenth birthday saw him for war depart,
Even before that war was yet declared –
A volunteer, with career robbed of start
By six long years and more so fully snared.
Fortune smiled more kindly on the three of us
Who made our way so much more easily;
And for his minus we had gained the plus,
For us life's chances came more readily.
Throughout he did rejoice at our success:
No man's envy could ever be the less.

75

Indignation all charity destroys
And robs the soul of that which matters most:
It shatters kindness and mercy decoys,
Panders to pride and sees not what is lost.
Self-righteousness the subtlest poison is,
Convincing conscience harshness is the right,
Sure we proclaim God's justice, yet 'tis not His –
Insights we posture reflect twisted light.
We see not self-importance in our stance
And think we have sound wisdom to pronounce
And our conceits fail signally to lance
And let the cubs of anger fiercely pounce.
Pontification's urge it's wise to quell:
Kindly forbearance best breeds sweetness' spell.

76

Some special women remain girls through life
However many decades pass them by:
They seem to blunt down age's sharpest knife,
And wrinkling just conspires to beautify.
Though outer tissue may less supple grow
And colours fade to so much gentler hue,
The eyes can muster deep alluring glow,
Adding spice to Nature's so special brew,
And youthful poise turns to a graceful grace
Whilst posture and gait conquer life's decline
And caring, loving lines enhance the face
And twinkling smiles exalt the superfine.
If you assert that I am starry-eyed,
I know she'd make a glorious, beauteous bride.

77

Most humans resent unjust harm to them,
Much less keen to weigh their own injustice:
Only blessed spirits their anger stem,
Spurning the fools who with resentment dice.
I knew a man with cause to feel aggrieved:
Just one of three prized scholarships he won
Ere his father of him the chance relieved,
For cost of uniform denied his son.
The feckless father renounced wife and home:
Never complaining, the son battled through,
Supporting home, taking life as it might come,
Ever positive, principled and true.
He never envied, never grudged success,
E'er rejoicing to see others progress.

78

I used to pray for what I needful thought,
So sure I knew what was the happy end,
In human imperfection blindly caught,
Not accepting God as all-knowing friend.
The minds we have can fine achievements forge,
Sound solutions and discoveries make,
And help us through life's deeply scrambling gorge,
And great artistic ventures undertake.
Yet all these aptitudes a weakness hold:
Overconfidence proud frailties begets,
Leading to assumptions perversely bold,
Sure of the future from fault-born mindsets.
So now I pray not for earthly outcome:
God alone knows how best to bring us home.

79

Why accept a fraction when there's a whole?
Rationality and reason fall short
If you elect to circumvent the pole,
Taking false refuge in your sense-based fort.
The term 'infinity' clearly deters,
Sounds intellectual, unattainable;
But if it's 'whole' to which debate refers
Do 'parts' alone remain discussable?
Such parts are ever larger seen to grow
As e'er expanding universe depicts,
Save those we find acutely smaller show
In this world's so strange outward-inward mix.
Till Nature ends, whatever science saith,
I'll stick to my more satisfying faith.

80

Wail not for your religion's sad demise,
The dire decline of priestly labourers.
Holiness is ne'er built on useless sighs
Nor helped by cries from aimless clamourers.
To us, the vineyard is God-committed:
Acts and omissions partake of treason,
All our behaviour debased or fitted,
Too oft oblivious good has no season.
Ignore not then the generous instinct
Or turn away from others' sad distress;
Allow not your actions to be self-linked,
But let humanity your kindness bless.
Write on your hearts, be it in prose or rhyme
These are the chronicles of wasted time.

81

All human insights shortcomings suffer:
Judgements sound-seeming lead too oft astray,
So making the paths of others rougher
And failing to see when black and white are grey.
Spouses' dependence oft uneven grows
As age and weakness spawn different needs,
So one more active greater caring shows
And then dependence on dependence feeds.
When one dies, reactions may sadly err:
Greater concern the one dependent gains,
But often draws in another carer –
Who's to say carer suffers lesser pains?
Be cautious in ascribing grief's sad cost:
The carers have their loving focus lost.

82

Anniversaries, death-destroyed, bite hard:
Gold mercilessly turns itself to dross
And pain slips noiselessly within the guard,
Making all pleasure into candyfloss.
Three years and more of aching gap have passed,
A gentle aching as befits her soul,
Gently bidding me forward looks to cast,
Honouring her with truly smiling role.
Such smiling would, you'd think, enhance the pain,
But gentleness was gentle legacy
And she would judge unceasing mourning vain,
Regarding it as love's apostasy.
That behest I still will strive to honour,
Though life is stripped of most taste and colour.

83

The urge to love, the urge to give survive
The knowing that one's ardour's not returned,
Instincts keeping love powerfully alive,
Fuelling the hearth in which one's love is burned.
Rejection at least dispels hints of bribe
And proclaims the loving surely selfless,
Lest any should guile to one's gifts ascribe,
Charging one with base deviousness.
It further means that taking bears no guilt,
For taking assuages the giver's pain
With no assumptions thereby built;
Thus each accorded is a guiltless gain.
When the giving is with true loving touch,
The taking is a giving just as much.

84

Symbol of loss and pain, the broken heart,
Withholding of that magical response,
Rich in metaphor, darling child of art,
Which within the soul ardour did ensconce.
When young, for years I knew the symptoms well,
Bruised yearning, raw gaping listlessness,
Struggling lest bitterness should cast its spell,
So powerless deep feeling to express.
And, when old, the selfsame torment ensues,
Keeping standards up and playing jester
Ne'er to embarrass others as one rues
Pangs of love and memories that fester.
I'm left crushed where once passion burned,
The empty aching of love unreturned.

85

Grab, grab, grab, from your cold grey hearts, ye souls,
Ne'er fail to grasp where your fancy beckons,
Nor pleasures forsake when for you fortune rolls,
Nor ponder the bill that Heaven reckons.
How fearsome to envisage losing out
And think that others may have more than you,
Or there's a trough that's never felt your snout –
Nor doubt a pampered will should see you through!
All generous and kindly instincts crush;
Never believe virtue is aught but odd
Or think that beauty is worth more than plush –
Evade the awkwardness of knowing God.
Ne'er detect you live on a shallow shoal
Or recognise yourself as Orwell's prole.

86

So oft I wonder at what artists grasp
And capture it two-dimensionally,
So gently coaxing out of Nature's clasp
What poor we would miss pathetically.
How privileged we who in Lakeland dwell,
Savouring beauty in each step we take,
Hard-pressed for words that might such splendour tell –
E'en cameras deep images cannot make.
But then a blessed spirit captures gold
And thus shows character as well as shape,
Determined for beauty, but never bold,
Just immortalising a known landscape.
So many paintings – who'd want greater fill?
Until one sees the magic wrought by Jill.

87

We live in times when rights are all the rage
As if they were an unmixed happiness
And paved the way unto a golden age,
Leaving all humans thereby questionless.
Yet rights envisage other persons' acts:
Force they have not lest others duties owe –
Rights in Fairyland dealing not in facts,
While high-flown wording cannot content show.
Only one right, I'll own, true substance has –
The right to know just what one's duties are:
That's how civilisation ever was,
With duty for law its sole guiding star.
View not your rights as beguiling beauty:
Truest joy remains the fruit of duty.

88

Treat not your loving as alternative,
As if one can apportion out one's heart:
Genuine love must be cumulative –
Cancel no love, another one to start.
Loving wrinkles whene'er it hinders growth:
Its only nature is to overflow
Whether within the solemn marriage oath
Or to the passing strangers as they go.
Howe'er great the love, greater it can be:
Love for one, denial for another
Trample down honest generosity
And instincts for good unwisely smother.
Longing to be loved is ne'er satisfied
Until your loving spreads itself worldwide.

89

That God is love bestrides all Christian thought
And love prescribes that loving finds its base.
Love alone is in finite bonds not caught
And ever shows a gently smiling face.
The never-fading battleground of life
Is where love contends 'gainst grasping self –
Harsh contention 'twixt love's balm and self's knife,
Sweet medicine and poison from off hell's shelf.
All this humanity acknowledge must
And yet clings fast to its sad selfishness,
Choosing disharmony 'fore loving trust
And dubbing God's providence flavourless.
God moves, they say, in mysterious ways:
There's mystery only on our selfish days.

90

Who can resist the bluebell's cheering charm,
Joyfully enriching the country scene,
Able the greyest cynic to disarm
With lovely, lively mix of blue and green?
The daffodil rightly Dora's Field owns,
Only to see the bluebell follow on,
Each to inject sweet beauty in our bones,
Still haunting when both their flowers have gone.
Yet Scotland can a fairer rival claim –
Or so I judge on mountainside and lane,
Close victor in Nature's enchanting game –
How could either ever meet with disdain?
Why England loves its choice I know full well,
But cherish best the delicate harebell.

91

In Jenbach town I learnt a lesson true
Which clever minds too readily dismiss:
For simple things there's special homage due –
Lowly pursuits engender healing bliss.
Tyrol's youth endowed us with humble charm,
Lavished on us a rustic culture rich,
Scorning sophistication's cruel arm,
Preferring candour's honest needle's stitch.
While thrusting youth enthrones self's altar bare
And seeks fulfilment in a carnal chase,
These joyous dancers gave us lilting fare
That made our hearts awake and pulses race.
Never despise such unflattered treasure,
But tune your souls to sweet ländler's measure.

92

A passing friendship sounds a paltry term:
A lasting one sustains a treasured brace;
And yet, depth, not length, makes our loving firm
And fleeting warmth may have a hallowed place.
A fortnight only was our bonding ground
Where mutual rapport demanded birth
And sneer and pettiness were never found
And each responded to the other's worth.
Through Brig, Luzern, Chur, Jenbach united
We knew re-meeting was but smallest chance,
But knew too our bond would be unblighted
And we were richer for such circumstance.
There lasted mirth and kindness all that while
And we were friends who ne'er forwent a smile.

93

Injustice comes in many tragic forms:
Classed 'ex-young lady' is by far the worst.
It merits tantrums and the fiercest storms
And crushes egos, leaving self-love burst.
The years run by, the hurt grows deeper still:
In retrospect 'young lady's' charm has gone,
Love's nomenclature has lost all its thrill,
With joy of living cruelly undone.
No therapy, no counselling can save
The shattered soul, nor yet the bludgeoned heart.
What future beckons but the bleakest grave?
The power has gone to sire life's restart.
Howe'er, let her one sparkling smile unfurl,
Young lady gone, we have the sweetest girl.

94

By Garda's shore we forged a friendship fine –
Experience told us it would fleeting be:
Yet e'en speed fades when depth and warmth combine,
Enabling us to find a richer we.
For all the beauty in our brave surround
A beauty too in friendly bonds we find,
While sweet emotions in our hearts abound
And gentle comradeship delights the mind.
And one thing completes the bliss we feel –
A ministering angel of our own
To give our drifting vessel surer keel:
If clouds obtrude, we have our splendid Dawn.
One thought we hug as our adventure ends:
We laughed, we joked, but – best of all – were friends.

95

We came together on a holiday,
With fun and joy amidst our timid hopes,
But knowing well such times skate fast away,
So soon sealed up within life's envelopes.
Friendship's gentle bonds haphazardly grew
As Vienna, Budapest and Prague conspired
Round us their special magic to imbue,
While undetected sweetest chains were fired.
Surest cement our glee in Nature's trowel,
We soundly built our treasured comradeship,
That tender bonding that ne'er seeks avowal,
But knows full well love's coinage not to clip.
Bright souls their lustre do forever give:
Know then, their rich warmth will as long survive.

96

So late I knew him, in declining time,
Seeing the man with grim Death taking guard;
For me just fleeting glance of that man's prime
'Fore illness sadly took him for its ward.
Yet, to be sweet when life's force swaggers high
Is easy: judge him better in decline.
'Twas then we saw his prime concealed no lie:
His soul was honest, kind and superfine.
But even that was not the sum of him:
Joy, glee and playful mischief ever glowed
Through eyes that sparkled to the very brim:
A happy man who happiness bestowed.
And if in dying pain and bleakness grew,
The sweetness, love and goodness still shone through.

97

Some claim the right to die in dignity
And seek indignity in circumstance,
As if life's riches lie just in pity
And suffering does not our selves enhance.
My heart has bled to see loved ones decline,
To see them endure pain, fear and squalor,
And wished their passion could instead be mine,
Whilst glory seeing in quiet valour.
'Twas then we measured out their real worth
And felt our love at least escaped the mean,
And put our hope in Heaven's sweet rebirth,
Where life's devotion stays forever green.
If this were wrong our faith would be undone,
But we know better, and await God's sun.

98

How sadly do we mangle beauteous words
And make them trite, banal and sugary!
No longer can they strike harmonious chords
Or soothe the heart when steeped in misery.
Saddest of all these bludgeoned words is 'nice':
'Nice phrase', 'nice shot', 'nice judgement' still enthuse
The minds that value weigh, ignoring price,
And shudder in ire at such rank abuse.
For he was nice in conduct, mien and soul,
In humour, kindness, deftness and address.
Such niceness failed not with Death's drumbeat roll,
But gently the greater grew, not the less.
All this augments our pain to near despair,
Save he was noble, fine and passing fair.

99

Some men you warm to as the years go on:
Some other few you know their worth straightway.
And such a man was he – life's favoured son
Who lightened lives and banished darkling day.
Lucky those who knew him long and deeply:
A merry friend, a kindly soul, a gem
That still shone bright as life expired steeply:
All loved him well as he in turn loved them.
Full genuine his warmth, his word, his love,
He stood foursquare upon the stage of life:
Faithful to loved ones and to his God above,
And simply joyous in a world of strife.
We are the losers with such grievous loss:
No part of him could ever pass as dross.

100

We went an-eating to the Strickland Arms,
Deferring sorrow for an evening's fun.
Our loved one dead would surely clap his palms
To know we loved too well his joy to shun.
Oh, yes! A shadow we could sense full well
And scorned to feign it was not in our hearts;
But shadows do not always coldness spell
Nor bring despair within our deepest parts.
He was a man of laugh and smile and gave
Full measure to us all throughout his life:
He would reject such vict'ry to the grave
And bless our meal with gentle humour rife.
Though bittersweet our evening had to be
His sweetness to the fest did hold the key.

101

The mysteries of life pervade the soul
With death the sole provider of true test:
Only in its light can one call life's roll
And sift the transient from out the best.
For humankind can shine in fertile field
And prance bold upon bravely sparkling stage,
But plenty can oft meagre harvest yield
And aftersight belie a golden age.
A marriage too can seem to ride on high,
Evoking envy in the saddened breast
Till shallowness piles crudely sigh on sigh
And what seemed greatest leaks out bleakest least.
Contrast to that best witness to arouse,
The tender spirit of the dying spouse.

102

When first I knew him, full well I liked him;
  Repute confirmed my judgement of the man.
Here was one who e'er dwelt on laughter's rim,
But never hurt as often others can.
When illness struck and held him in its sway
I knew him better and saw his mettle clear:
Here was courage and patience all the day,
Light'ning loads of those who so held him dear.
Life was the richer for his gentle role,
Consideration was his constant mark,
The wasted body held a wid'ning soul
And spirit triumphed over gathering dark.
The pain and weakness conquered in the end,
And yet he was a lovely, loving friend.

103

I love her late, but love her truly deep.
The lines of age her beauty do enhance:
That beauty always makes my heart to leap,
Her hair exalts while sparkling eyes do dance.
Youth may scoff and seasoned heads dispense scorn
That hearts so old should harbour 'passioned dreams,
And loving instincts be so full reborn –
Aphrodite's sun share with age its beams.
Her gentle soul and tender heart endear,
All unconscious of her so precious worth,
While others' sorrows she will staunchly bear
And prove long years do not entail love's dearth.
Years drop away and teen-age storms the heart:
Once more, the pain is bliss from Cupid's dart.

104

The more I know you, the more I love you.
That has been so throughout all history:
Surveying gaze needs time for inmost true,
Fully to savour love's deep mystery.
The instant glory captures untrained eyes,
Such glory so deserves such servitude,
But subtler shades the heart must realise:
There's more to loving than just pulchritude.
The prompting heart may sore lament missed past
And wonder how your springtime beauty shone
And curse the law that makes love's steps speed fast
And rue love's years will all too soon be gone.
Your beauty now's the earning of your life:
It is that beauty I would take for wife.

105

A song of wonder is my love for thee.
How couldst thou still such loveliness preserve?
How shelter it from life's encroaching sea
And turgid stolidness so sharp unnerve?
Whene'er I look I long to look once more.
Such feast is proof 'gainst indigestion's claim
And sating self merely conserves the core
Of all the sweetness that bedecks thy name.
I marvel at the soaring of my soul,
So humdrum the poor musings of my mind,
Striving so hard to 'scape the jester's role
And for thy glory aptest words to find.
Forgive thy troubadour his awkwardness:
Thy splendour far outruns what tongues express.

106

I scanned the list of virtues I loved best
And found them all in my sweet lovely lass,
Not forcefully displayed with garish crest,
But gently hinted as the greens of grass.
A humble meekness with a courage sure,
A tenderness linked with a caring heart,
A sweetness sprung from soul forever pure,
No fierceness there, save on a victim's part;
Elegance of mind matching style in dress,
A simple wisdom in a modest head,
A prayerful honesty that doth impress,
An utter goodness, with all envy shed.
Beauty of soul, as of God's countryside,
A worth unsung she'll ever seek to hide.

107

I love, and love, and love, and still I love
And wonder at the workings of my heart,
Exulting wildly in my treasure trove
As if from stumbling on a pirate's chart.
I, so aged, my fervour find so strange:
How could I youth's frenzy so recapture,
Full sure its strength will now not ever change,
Captive sentenced to eternal rapture?
I'll praise the emptiness that went before
And made such contrast with my blissful now:
Dire want becoming swiftly richest store,
Just leaving me on quest to figure how;
And should I seek to find the reason why,
I only need survey my darling's eye.

108

Her ageless beauty does my mind perplex:
Lines there are, and skin youth's full bloom has lost,
Yet she remains the fairest of her sex
For lines of love do capture beauty most.
Alas, I never saw that splendid youth,
The full bright colours of her maiden hair,
The pearly innocence that's ne'er uncouth
And early charm that any heart would tear.
But hair responds: its peerless white so fine
With careless care so richly flowing free;
And eyes that sparkle like a matchless wine,
Ne'er to entrap, just making squalor flee.
How can this be, I am left to ponder,
Save that I am lost in endless wonder.

109

Yea or nay? The age-old questions madden:
Does she me like or merely tolerate?
And deeper yet can such question sadden
When loving 'tis that I do contemplate.
Such clear questions cannot wisdom answer,
Weighing evidence dispassionately?
How can it so when, like whirling dancer,
There's no base on which to judge sedately?
The smile, the frown, the laugh, the even blank,
Haphazardly o'erturn all thinking's law:
There's no sweet certainty on which to bank
As one so tries that chilling doubt to thaw.
I'm left knowing what all hist'ry has told:
There's no escape betwixt the hot and cold.

110

Those who would judge should first their vision test.
The world e'er seeks the confident to boost
And treat them always as by fortune blest
So they can strut, from shame and pity loosed.
The meek and humble are by contrast squashed,
So sadly robbed of all due scope to shine
And by their inward doubting harshly lashed,
Made to believe that they have nothing fine.
And what's the price we now have all to pay?
The thrusting ride high, flushed with easy win,
Grabbing the world's repute and wealth and sway,
The shy left aimless with but guerdon thin.
One dear girl does this tragedy redress:
Heaven depends on such soft-tuned sweetness.

111

I never looked to love thee, just to aid:
Thy stately beauty held me not in thrall
Till I glimpsed the shy, sparkling inner maid
Peeping out from behind convention's wall.
No urge to possess, just foster, cherish,
Bring forth her lustre to this world of grey,
On her full tenderness fondly lavish,
Gently subject all loving to her sway.
Sophistication lost all chance to rule
And simple truths my captured heart bestrode
And all who doubted risked the name of fool,
Adrift, without the key to loving's code.
The truest love gives just one hint of proof:
It pours out, ensuring self stands aloof.

112

My love is wholesome: what strange term, you'll say.
Pretty, charming, lovely and beauteous, yes,
But where is romance with a word so grey?
What sound for lips to conjure sweet caress?
Yet 'wholesome' marks the beauty of the soul –
Clear, clean, straightforward, and with nothing gross,
Tender, considerate, a constant pole
On compass sound, no superficial gloss,
Caring, loving, modest and sweetly kind,
With principle her ever-guiding light,
Seeking sound sense in place of twisted mind,
And dedicated always to the right.
Beauty is there to touch, to hear, to see,
But under all deepest integrity.

113

I seek for judgement, find it not within:
Intelligence I have, discretion lack.
What price the brilliance when the wisdom's thin,
The shooting star that never cometh back?
The world will ever fête the clever brain,
Yet rarely rate the merit of sound sense.
But if the brain pursues a fruitless lane,
'Tis only wisdom that can rescue thence.
A lass, as ever, gives the guidance due
Gently restraining the hasty male surge
When all his cogitation goes askew,
Fails to detect his faulty thinking's urge.
Thankful then, I praise her dear discerning:
Her wisdom countermands my errant learning.

114

Show me a man of passion, love and fire
Whom carnal impulse nearly holds in thrall,
Who yet his lady dear full loves to squire,
Chains up desire and makes her sweetness all.
I'll show you then that love is truly true
And he is master of his inner self.
His is a potion from a loving brew
Which Venus takes from off her topmost shelf.
All lurid fantasy is kept in check
To make the loving fortress of respect,
And loved one such as angels strive to deck
With innocence that squarely stands erect.
Love is not love when trace of guilt defiles
Or honest modesty succumbs to wiles.

115

What means she to my arid, aching soul?
A kindness and a sweetness and a balm,
A gentle granting, gentle as a foal,
Moist'ning my desert with soft, dew-borne calm.
There is no place for words of passion now,
Just simple messages of friendship deep,
Forbidding solitariness to grow
Though tears may strive their sorry tale to peep.
'Twas her dearness which made my lack so clear
And disinterred male need for female grace
And brought to sterile flatness welcome cheer,
With tender smiles my greyest clouds to chase.
And thus her sweetness will forever bring
A precious bloom that is a golden thing.

116

A very goddess, stately, grand and fine –
Grey word, deportment, but still fits so well,
With all the value of a vintage wine –
The word that cometh surely is not belle.
I wonder at the majesty of her
Enchained within her ageless beauty's bond,
Loveliness that knows not how to falter,
Enslaving with no need for witch's wand.
And yet, 'twas not that set my heart afire:
Beauty I recognised, but no knee bent,
It was the sudden smile made me her squire,
The uncrushed sparkle that me crashing sent.
Tho' 'tis her splendour holds my heart in fee,
She my soul conquered with her gleam of glee.

117

She was a Jewish maid who loved so deep
And sang to magnify her dearest Lord,
A lass with greatest cause to stand and weep
With heart transfixed by life's relentless sword.
She was just one within a chosen line,
Who knew the law, the prophets and the psalms
And loved that law and cherished God's design,
Be it her Son's scourging or brandished palms.
What better advocate than one so hurt,
Whose grief's a measure for all human woe,
Who knew abasement, yet escaped all dirt
And ne'er sought a place save amidst the low.
A sweet, sad title, Our Queen of Sorrows,
God's guarantee for everlasting morrows.

118

The truest love presents a cruel bill:
Dying spouse views survivor's growing grief;
Survivor lives on with sad, wilting will,
Future too long, the years of bliss too brief.
Anniversaries exact a special toll,
Trampling joyous memories into dust:
The first the bleakest for the mourning soul,
Repressing tears as custom says one must.
Unreality stalks the tortured heart,
The how and why baffling the groping mind,
As certainties of union all depart
And threads of life so painfully unwind.
Now shrouded fast within a cloud of grey,
Just sweet remembrance marks the festal day.

119

The lure of riches and the hint of gold
Oft occupy a wistful woman's thoughts,
So sadly unaware her soul is sold
And her calculations made up of noughts.
Blessed then the girl whom simple things do charm,
Seeing her gold in shining buttercups
And riches in the skilful craftsman's arm,
Gently offsetting downs against life's ups,
When one can make a daisy chain from life,
Taking delight in flowers' finery,
The while disdaining self-love's inward strife,
Full proof 'gainst this world's fickle flattery.
The saddest birthday this for her must be,
But we descry sweetest simplicity.

120

The question springs, 'why she so special was?'
Other women are sweet and beautiful
With charms that womankind so richly has
And to the laws of love are dutiful.
Ne'er unkindly was that effervescence
Nor harsh or sour that joyous laughter's ring,
With modesty that masked intelligence
Without restraint on her gentle loving;
And over all complete integrity,
Not blazoned, but deeply, quietly built:
Unbowed by official iniquity,
She maintained a faith that would never wilt.
Darling nature on a character sound,
She was a treasure that's so seldom found.

121

Let forgiveness be your second nature
And it will make your first the best:
Lofty indignation grants not stature,
It merely succeeds real love to arrest.
Judging's glamour is just self-importance:
Can the guilty truly weigh up the guilt,
Or fairly claim the one sure sifter's stance
And think justice is on detection built?
The law can never even out all wrongs
Or hope to punish ev'ry wrongdoer:
Thinking it can imparity prolongs,
Nor ever makes this world's rogues the fewer.
Unless there's judgement from an all-wise God,
Life's greatest villains will escape dry-shod.

122

Oh, why should I not die instead of him?
I make no judgement on intrinsic worth,
Just know we stand on love's and loving's rim
And on the pain and loss of sorrow's birth.
Useless question amidst sore bursting hearts,
We know too well the answer's high above:
Life's patchwork lies far beyond its parts
And moral insights feel no fitting glove.
The robbery of death paints rosily,
Stoutly denying existence of bale,
Insisting life would go on cosily
And bliss in age would surely never fail.
Heaven knows when life's judging best takes place:
And that's high season for our gaining grace.

123

Most dangerous sin is withholding love:
Even murder can be a lesser crime,
For anger may spring from a wounded move –
Only meanness of heart persists through time.
Stifling out loving turns all natures sour
And crushes instincts to be generous,
Op'ning all doors to unlovely rancour
And dark'ning down all that is luminous.
The void's that left is filled alone by self
And self-pampered self must claim priority,
Blind to the spirit's all-malignant elf,
Love's semblance dripping towards humanity;
Think never such polite indifference
Can confer least hint of vital conscience.

124

Love ne'er stands still nor lasts in pickled state:
It ever grows, it ever spreads its realm,
Or else the maggot self will blight its fate,
For outward look must he who holds love's helm.
Paramountcy loved ones can fairly claim,
But only whilst absorption is denied:
A golden conduit sprung from Fortune's Dame
Must ever be the lovers' truest pride.
The world's a loveless desert for our race
Which fails to see that love is limitless,
Chill souls that fearfully blot out love's face,
Seeing not containing love is witless.
Fail not then to give your love boundless flow,
For love confined is never fit to grow.

125

True testament of love comes not from death,
The passioned clinging to the sawn-off life:
The story lives within the loving breath,
The golden legacy of man or wife.
Expanded heart expansion still must know,
The craft of loving never gone to waste:
All else may stagger, let not loving slow,
Lest deepest love finds its true truth defaced.
The heart is torn, the soul is deeply bruised,
The mind cries out, 'Avoid again such pain!'
Beware, true loving ne'er must be abused:
Reward thy love – through it its heights attain.
Death's stolen the centre of our being –
Forbid it should send our loving fleeing.

126

Love satisfies, but only just so far,
Unless the loving being loved outruns:
Let love exude lest self such love may mar,
Leaving lover and loved disbalanced ones.
He who seeks scales for love imprisoned is
Within the walls of unlovely conceit,
Allotting too sharply the hers and his,
Pacing all out with dully measured feet.
Instead, each loving touch uncounted be:
With calculation gone, let instinct rule,
For loving's dead when mind extorts a fee
And craves response too evenly to school.
Never too sparsely set to sow love's seed,
Just learn to recognise the needful need.

127

Crave not death, howe'er burdensome is life;
Others there are whose burdens you may lift,
Light'ning their bleakness or soothing their strife –
A willing tongue can deftly drabness shift:
That in this world sole sadness' recompense,
It makes the suffering less hard to bear
However little it may seem sound sense
Or tell the heart that there is healing there.
That heart the aching losses will still feel
Where death or rejection has deadheaded
The precious blossoms of life's richest weal
And made all one's steps so harshly leaded.
This alone can temper life's sparse decline
And hew some comfort from earth's deepest mine.

128

It is the sharing that I miss so much:
Bewitching sunsets and the stars of night,
Whispered nothings holding the richest touch,
Little consequence, yet surest delight.
What would be trifling, bathed in love's outflow,
Became the glory of our wedded tie,
That silent bonding that only spouses know
With playful fancies that will tell no lie.
We took the pluses and the minuses
And from both together forged our pairing,
Filled with sweetness and despising fusses –
Such is the essence of all true sharing.
But now, whate'er the arguments deployed,
The loss of sharing leaves my living void.

129

The cruel banishment from all that's dear,
  The loved one's death, or else her lasting no:
Where boldness strode there's now just cold and fear,
Useless attempts to shield from deadly blow.
They say that tears can grant the heart respite,
But mine would merely irrigate the hurt,
For I know well 'gainst loss I cannot fight –
Fate's answer is so brutal and so curt.
I am but one of many million souls,
Perhaps my pain can earn for some relief
In Heaven's courts, that must impose such tolls
To give a meaning to our sure belief.
That solace is, but leavens not the pain:
The baiting void will e'er its rasp retain.

130

Oh! We were eight, but now a sorry five,
My love and I the last to join the set,
But six equal first would us not deprive,
For all of us owed each a joyous debt.
A golden sunlike glow through eight years shone:
Liz died, and then the gold of autumn came,
We had lost an irreplaceable one –
There was now touch of sadly halting lame.
My Pauline died, our dear John then followed,
Leaving us with quixotic pot-pourri,
That haunting mixture of joys sharp hollowed,
Happy mem'ries, but so much less of glee.
It is of course just as Nature conspires –
We're left the embers of spluttering fires.

131

Count not the sins that you have not committed,
Nor overlook the very ones you have:
Heaven's not so easily outwitted
And that's blind alley for your soul to save.
Celestial ledgers look towards the heart,
Not towards points above and beneath a line.
Scale of loving sets good and bad apart –
Self-love victorious e'er thwarts what's divine.
Who concentrates just on avoiding wrong
Can never so sustain the negative:
Who loves, who gives, to Heaven doth belong
And with the angels surely learns to live.
This lonely plea would scarce in Heaven pass,
'I never coveted my neighbour's ass.'

132

Though through life we great sinnings may avoid,
We court imperfection at ev'ry turn.
Our good intentions are too oft decoyed
As moral values we unwitting spurn.
Mean acts we judge as mere peccadilloes,
Omitted kindness no cause to worry;
Let's drift as self-will's breeze alluring blows
And rids us of need for feeling sorry –
Hell smiles discreetly at the fools we are:
Why interfere when self can all sense defy?
Our seeming bliss no more than tarnished star,
Instincts for good bartered for getting by.
Asked what it is that Heaven most respects,
Angels cry, '*Caritas Suprema Lex.*'

133

Appetites sustain our wondrous human frame,
Securing the future as much as now,
Allowing genes to play their magic game,
Tender mix of the what, the why, the how.
We're not just brother's keeper, but our child's,
From e'en before an act of procreation
As our ev'ry act that child's nature builds,
Precious fruit of genetic donation;
With impulse founded on mad ecstasy
To ensure the core ingredient of love –
Heaven's endowment from earth's embassy,
The troth of flesh, all hallowed from above.
If thou wouldst holiness in love ensconce,
Match responsibility to response.

134

I have not a desert ever trodden,
But felt within its tow'ring emptiness,
Known my soul's landscape so bleakly sodden
With unshed tears of sheer unhappiness.
I've known the knife, I've known the rasp of love
Lingering on without hope of return;
I've known fate resilience rudely remove
And felt passion's fierce inner icy burn.
I've known the prison of keep wondering why,
Known musings of delight falsely intrude,
Then seen my loving perched upon a sigh
That does earthly bliss so sharply preclude;
But in my heart I sadly recognise
It is such pain that makes our soul more wise.

135

Concept of lady so intently shirked,
Crushed out on the sad altar of self-love:
No more the craft of elegance fine worked,
Sacrificed in a world of glare and shove.
Shallow beautifying commands the field
If beauty e'er lies in expensive aids
As tawdry products their sad thraldom wield:
Whate'er happened to demure, pretty maids?
Oh, yes! There's force in all cosmetic lure,
But artifice e'er sends a later bill,
Forcing exchange of false array for pure,
Thrusting temptations on a wilting will.
Be not trapped into expensive living:
Truest beauty lies in gentle giving.

136

Pity those who the humble donkey scorn,
See no appeal in lowly gentleness,
Appreciate not the charm of eyes forlorn,
Never discover how long ears may bless.
Oh, what a name can nobility sound!
Acclaim lion and tiger do command,
And which on horse and eagle does redound
For all with true dignity must e'er stand.
But is this truth so undeniable?
Does their merit outrun their noble stance?
Or their prey them adjudge reliable?
Is all fine worth found just in courtly dance?
Happiness in life demands the steady –
I find true sweetness in dearest Neddy.

137

No man I know with better cause to boast,
But boasting to his nature is untrue.
Nor content could he be through life to coast,
He knows too well the price to virtue due.
So many talents, so great modesty,
Strength of mind with subtle humour wedded,
Deeming deceit as cruel travesty,
With unbragged honour so deep imbedded.
Happy those many who can call him friend,
All those he knows who have integrity:
They know his principles he'd never bend
Nor for the piteous stint his pity.
But all this does not define the whole:
There lies beneath the deeply loving soul.

138

So oft bereavement sombres loving hearts,
Yet still the sudden spark can them enthuse,
As loneliness its sour conquest departs
And solid goodness briefly sports its dues.
For him gregariousness held little charm,
But those he loved he filled with sparkling joy:
His wit so sharp never inflicted harm
And his shy smile could e'er our spirits buoy.
His roots, his times acuity confined,
So intellect was forced to humbler roles.
Yet brilliance was with shrewdness close combined
And there was warmth within the smould'ring coals.
His was a mind bedecked with finery,
But we'll recall the sweetness and the glee.

139 – Epilogue

Be sparing with your tears upon my death:
Life its tally has of sorrows and joys;
Mine had a greater share of fortune's breath,
Blest with a nature that my spirit buoys.
The happy days outnumbered those of gloom,
Pain and loss bit deep, but enriched my heart,
Whilst shadows ne'er depressed to point of doom,
And jest and smiling formed my soul's rampart.
The middle years were happiest of all,
But first and last were never reft of balm,
And fate's best cleansing comes from show'ry squall
And life was never traced for endless calm.
Mixed feelings now bedeck my worldly scene:
Life's drearer now than when the leaves were green.

140 – Envoi

Ask not from me what my sonnets may mean,
They mean whate'er the reader makes of them:
Scattered petals with some's distinctive sheen
Or dross that others will with joy condemn.
Some when I writ I thought I knew their sense,
Only now to puzzle unto defeat,
But still for some they may a spark dispense:
If so, perhaps there's merit there to greet.
The very confines of just fourteen lines
Impose most modest rein to soaring thought –
Which some may welcome like some heady wines,
Others reject: so just view this poor message wrought
Maund'rings of one who love could scarce inspire,
But bore within its priceless, scorching fire.

Notes

Sonnet Writing

Although I studied English poetry at school back in the 1940s, I did not then or for many years later attempt to compose any myself. I do recall penning a few juvenile pieces of Latin verse for schoolboy fun, but I cannot envisage their having had any merit: I just loved Latin, and Catullus's ode on his return to Italy to honour his brother's ashes has remained my favourite poem, along with Shakespeare's sonnets and Gray's 'Elegy'. It was only in the 1980s that I became enthusiastic about sonnets and read Shakespeare's in real detail. I put together a half-dozen or so of my own for individuals among my students at Nottingham University, and they seemed to appreciate them. I cannot find copies of them now, but I regard that as no great tragedy. [The Appendix which rounds off this volume is a response to a discovery made by chance as I was clearing out papers while I was finishing off these notes.]

It seems remarkably strange to me that I should now take up writing them in my seventies. Friends whose judgement and frankness I respect have encouraged me, even to the extent of pressing me to seek publication for the sonnets. I have my own liking for them, but feel incapable of judging what merit, if any, they contain. My one stimulus has been my belief that the messages which these efforts seek to get across may mean something to envisaged readers which they may feel of value to them. Perhaps it was my own experience of bereavement in losing a wonderful wife, which was followed two years after her death with the witnessing of another heartbreaking bereavement, that triggered what I have since written. Widows and widowers expressed appreciation of my bereavement sonnets, and that provided the stimulus to expand.

I can claim no organised, let alone expert or comprehensive study of the genre. I was aware of the differing rhyme patterns between the Petrarchian and the Spenserian or Shakespearean varieties, and went no further than dipping into basic anthologies and spasmodically consulting my now venerable *Oxford Companion to English Literature*. I was intrigued by Shakespeare's concentration on just the Spenserian form and by the apparent preponderance of Petrarch's rhyming system in all the subsequent great English poets' sonnets. Whilst full of admiration for those sonnets, and recognising the wonderful beauty and lyricism of the Petrarchian system, I find the Shakespearean form seems to suit my style of composition better, giving the final couplet a greater impact, I feel. It will be seen that I adopt that form in all the sonnets here: I have felt no temptation to go outside it.

Perhaps because I am such a novice I have avoided some of the latitudes of composition that Shakespeare adopts. In particular, I have sought to maintain a ten-syllable line throughout, although full of admiration for the aptness of his nine and eleven syllable departures; even so, a few, I have later discovered, seem to have crept in without apparent disaster! At the same time I have enthusiastically adopted his freedom of stress allocation, attenuating the old pentameter attribution almost shamelessly. The rhyming conventions I have endeavoured to observe very strictly: only very rarely have I succumbed to allowing a consonant to start the rhyme ending and always, I hope, because the effect seems to be particularly required. I also hope that use of alliteration has not been overdone and has always been apt.

I recognise that, not infrequently, I have consciously opted for words and forms that may quite fairly be regarded as antiquated. I hope I have not overdone it. In every case I found the usage suited what I wanted to convey and I hope it is more than mannerism. Thus here and there 'doth' and the like did seem to fit best – and to me, at least, still do after repeated rereading. I like to think it is not calculated archaism, but an acknowledgement of the vibrancy of over four hundred years of modern English. If it jars, I am very sorry – but unrepentant. Similarly, one or two metaphors occur more than once: 'Fortune's Dame' is an instance. I ask forgiveness if that offends, but it seemed to me, even after considerable thought, to be just as apt as when first used.

It will be seen how much I relish the challenge of compacting a theme or reflection into just fourteen lines. In most cases the first line or two or the final couplet come to mind and then dictate the rest, and the message is intended to be a unity. Here and there it may be detected that I have started with a theme and then allowed the 'message' to alter course. All I can say is that I did recognise each instance as it came out and found myself content at the outcome.

Finally, I have to admit that I do not readily find the sonnet a natural medium for humour, except perhaps for irony (which I have done my best to use sparingly, I hope). Only two – 35 and 93 – are entirely attempts at sustained, uncensorious humour and both use hyperbole gleefully. A sonnet, I feel, is not mortally harmed by an occasional giggle.

Individual Sonnets

As said in the Preface, 7 was written way back in May 2004, three months or so after Pauline's death. Its reception by its recipients was so kind as to incline me towards writing more, but it was nearly two years later that I set out to compose any. The first set written comprises 96 to 102. As the text should show, they celebrate the quiet dignity in dying of a very special and much admired man, and they were written for his widow. I hope the quality of the man comes over in the verses. I wish so much I had known him longer and better, but perhaps the lines will indicate how much he meant to so many people in our area of Cumbria. 101 was written months later as a sort of retrospect, while 102 had been written with the others, but not included with them originally: it was only later that I came across it and felt that, after all, it could stand with the others.

Sonnets 1 to 6 followed shortly after, stimulated by the emotions that writing the first set had evoked. 6 was written first of them and circulated among friends. Their enthusiasm for it prompted the fashioning of the other five. The ordering of them all was the result of a tentative judgement on how they might best be arranged for balance. I suspect it would have mattered little what order they took, so I have left them as I first compiled them. It will be seen that a number of later sonnets contain reprises about Pauline – 9, 25, 26, 30, 58, 61, 63 and 128 among them. Whatever their literary merit I trust the reason why she was so much loved and admired comes across.

8 is a tribute to Pauline's stepmother, Veronica, a gentle and very lovable soul who had taught art and craft before marrying Cyril in her mid-forties. Cyril was also a very special man, celebrated in sonnet 77. He had the distinction of having two wonderfully happy marriages, each of over thirty years' duration: Chrissie, his delightful first wife, was around fifteen years older than he was and Veronica was younger than him by roughly the same margin. I was so very lucky in my in-laws.

It will be apparent that a frequent theme of the sonnets is bereavement. They have helped me to work as best I may the implications and emotions of such events.

22 evokes a magical drive up and down Ullswater in April 2006: my companions and I were spellbound by the amazing beauty of the scene.

As indicated above, 35 and 93 (which, of the two, had in fact been written some months earlier) are the only two conceived as entirely humorous, with sustained mock hyperbole.

44 'celebrates' thoughts and emotions as I walked on Adelaide Hill overlooking Windermere and then along its shoreline below.

48 is a reflection on Luke 12: 22–31

54 tries to capture my response to the wonderful paintings of Georges de la Tour, the seventeenth-century painter from Lorraine. A few years previously I had seen a very fine programme on television about his work and had been greatly intrigued by his

genre, but it was a visit to the Louvre that had sparked off my enthusiasm for his work.

66 is a tribute to a very special saint – Bernadette of Lourdes. To Pauline and me she had been a wonderful inspiration, and I cannot help thinking that in her dying months especially Pauline reflected some of Bernadette's qualities.

72 is a reaction to a very remarkable schoolgirl faced with one of the most formidable of cancers and her fight to conduct a full and rich life in its shadow. Typically, she saw nothing exceptional in her response: we, however, did. She died a year or so after the sonnet was written. Her dying had become very distressing, yet also very sweet and uplifting, such was her courage and consideration: Janice was special.

73 relates to a five-day pilgrimage I took with four splendid ladies to Lourdes in May 2007. We were incredibly lucky to be booked on a plane with a pilgrimage party from Stalybridge. They and their priest, Father Bernard Forshaw, readily extended their wonderfully warm friendship to us without the least pushing. I hope the sonnet conveys at least some of the deep gratitude we owe them all.

74 recalls my eldest brother, Hugh, who died in 1997. Like Cyril in 77, he was an intensely lovable man, characterised by a total absence of envy or grudge and a total presence of friendliness and integrity.

As the text probably indicates, 82 relates to feelings on what would have been my golden wedding anniversary.

Those who know Tennyson's 'Break, break, break' – not so many nowadays as in my schooldays, I suspect – will perceive my debt to it in 85.

86 commemorates our love and admiration in Southern Lakeland for a remarkable painter and delightful woman, Jill Aldersley. I

am not alone in thinking that no artist has captured the beauty of the Lakes better. John Cornforth, her great friend and painting companion, shared that talent – he is celebrated in 137.

91 to 95 are Holiday Sonnets, written in respect of three holidays taken in 2006 and 2007. All three were trips provided by Great Rail Journeys, and each time I was blessed by being with a delightful group. The first three were written towards the end of a fortnight's Alpine Tour through Switzerland and Austria. 93 was written for a lady on the trip who light-heartedly told me how, when she and her husband were courting, she had accompanied him to a scientific conference at Cape Wrath: her designation on the accommodation listing was as his 'Young Lady'. When she returned to a later conference there after her marriage she was then designated on the list as 'ex-Young Lady': she was in no way deeply upset, but I felt the slight should be castigated with all due exaggeration. 94 relates to a holiday by Lake Garda and 95 to an 'Imperial Cities' trip to Vienna, Budapest and Prague.

96 to 102 have been discussed under 1 to 6.

103 to 116 should speak for themselves. Their subject is a very special lady, devoted to her late husband's memory.

117 is in honour of the Blessed Virgin Mary on her feast of Our Lady of Sorrows, 15 September.

For 119 I ascribe the title, 'Daisychain Girl'.

120 seeks to portray and honour a dear friend, Mary, a victim of a virulent leukaemia which killed her with shocking speed. She was a very special person.

122 records my reaction when it became clear that John Cornforth – despite the false dawns of several medical predictions – was going to die. That reaction was, I feel, entirely natural, though of course futile, as I hope the sonnet imparts. 137 was to

be my tribute to this most special of men, written during the at long last tranquil weeks of his gentle and loving dying.

130 recalls our immense good fortune when Pauline and I retired in 1992 to Ambleside in the Lake District to be enthusiastically welcomed into a lovely group of three very special couples; and then the sadness as the group gradually began to dissolve through death.

137 is referred to under 122.

138 is a tribute to John Rabjohns, a brilliant and much-loved Lancastrian, who began work in a coal mine and became an outstanding engineer. He was married to Liz, referred to in Sonnet 130, who matched him in lovability. The 'five' of that sonnet is now sadly reduced further to four.

140 brings to mind the reflection that perhaps poetry, like all true art, is not scored to be definitive.

Appendix

While I was close to completing the intended last section of this work – Notes – I suddenly found a folder containing three items. I was engaged in clearing up my study at the time. In the folder were three calligraphically inscribed poems. One was a short blank verse and very appealing poem entitled 'A New Strength' by a lady named Sue Mitchell, whom I am sure I have never met. The other two bore my name and title and were in strict Spenserian sonnet form.

The first of the two was entitled 'To Courage and To Love' and bore the date, December 1988. The other had the title 'Liberation' and was dated April 1990. Although in general I have an excellent memory – many of my friends would say an exceptional one – no amount of racking my brain has enabled me to recall my having written them or what may have triggered their writing. I have a vague feeling that I may have written them for a student or ex-student as a solace in time of stress or unhappiness. I might hazard a guess who this was, but I remain uncertain so I shall keep the name to myself.

I have no expertise whatever in the skill of allotting provenance to documents. Suffice it then that I can acknowledge that it is very likely I did write both at the times indicated. To my eyes at least, some of the wording and phrasing seems to have resemblance to my current sonnets, but I am very uncertain of the trains of thought that produced them.

All that said, I thought it might be of interest to readers to set them out in this appendix for whatever they may be worth.

> The depths of love are rooted not in joys:
> Joy is a selfish tenant of the soul,
> Endured pain the heart most surely buoys
> And conquered sorrows fill life's honoured roll.
> In vain in punishments we seek deserts,

But retribution rarely finds the mark,
And scorn deserved or undeserved hard hurts
And contempt's night is unrelieved dark.
If we consider we must recognise
We owe such debts for things unpunished.
Seldom the score of life justice defies,
And when it does for others we'll have bled.
The souls that suffer without bitterness
Are ones nobility will always bless.

★

When pain and woe so long have been our lot
And bleakness smothered all our joy and hope
And left our fragile confidence to rot,
There is so little room for aught but mope.
Yet as dark clouds contrast the blues of sky
And sweetness sweeter seems against the sour
The rearing anguish of captivity
Highlights the splendour that gilds freedom's hour.
Then runs the blood as free as ne'er before,
Then sings the heart with gladness ne'er yet known,
Then shackles loosed enrich our treasure store,
When long-earned joy from wretchedness is grown.
The darkest nightmare we can beaten deem
When liberty restores our scope to dream.

Printed in the United Kingdom by
Lightning Source UK Ltd., Milton Keynes
137117UK00001B/118-165/P